Dad's bum is SO SMELLY!

T0382083

Dawn McMillan

Illustrated by Ross Kinnaird

SCHOLASTIC

There's a rumble at our place …

An **explosion!** A *blast!*

Something is happening
and …
It's happening ***Fast!***

Dad's bum has

blown off!

With a *hiss* and a **roar**

it's gone out our front door …

Way **down** our path, out to the gate.

'Let's *chase* it, Dad, before it's too late!'

What a disaster! The bum's rolling **Faster!**
Off down the street past people we meet.

Rolling and rolling,
past old people strolling.

Past joggers in tights.

Past bikers with **lights**.

Past children **swinging**.

Past people **singing**.

Up hill and **down**, heading for town.

My heart is racing from **running** and **chasing!**

And now ...

The police have arrived!

They shout,

'**Stand aside!** We're coming through!

This bum on the loose will never do!

Not to mention it's a **smelly bum**, too!'

'This bum causes **crashes**, bad falls …

and splashes.

And with that smell on the breeze,

it's **wilting** the trees.'

'We'll have to **ARREST** it and take it to jail.
We police folk are clever, we never fail.
We'll catch this **bad bum** and lock it away.
A smelly and rolly bum must not go astray!'

But I think ...

My heart is **HEAVY**. I'm feeling **sad**.
I don't want a bum-free Dad.

Now Dad's getting **tired**.
He's done with the chase.
He's heading home
with a **frown** on his face.

But wait ...

What do I see? Can it be right?

I smell a smell and ...

Dad's bum is in **sight!**
It's **rolled** around the block.
It's out on its own.
Now it's **chasing** Dad
and we're heading for home!

The bum's getting closer.
It moves in for the catch ...

And **abracadabra,**
I see Dad's bum attach.
A miracle! A **wonder!**
Dad has his bum.

And he's all together,
with my **cousins** and Mum.
We're a family united.
I'm so **excited**.

No more bum worries.
No more bum **scurries**.
I give Dad a hug and
I say,

'Dad, please ...

'No more eating cabbage and peas!'

About the author

Hi, I'm Dawn McMillan. I'm from Waiomu, a small coastal village on the western side of the Coromandel Peninsula in New Zealand. I live with my husband Derek and our cat, Joyce. I write some sensible stories and lots of crazy stories! I love creating quirky characters and hope you enjoy reading about them.

About the illustrator

Hi. I'm Ross. I love to draw. When I'm not drawing, or being cross with my computer, I love most things involving the sea and nature. I also work from a little studio in my garden surrounded by birds and trees. I live in Auckland, New Zealand. I hope you like reading this book as much as I enjoyed illustrating it.

Published in the UK by Scholastic, 2024
1 London Bridge, London, SE1 9BG
Scholastic Ireland, 89E Lagan Road, Dublin Industrial Estate, Glasnevin, Dublin, D11 HP5F

SCHOLASTIC and associated logos are trademarks and/or registered trademarks of Scholastic Inc.

First published in New Zealand by Oratia Media, 2024

Text © Dawn McMillan, 2024
Illustrations © Ross Kinnaird, 2024

The right of Dawn McMillan and Ross Kinnaird to be identified as the author and illustrator of this work has been asserted by them under the Copyright, Designs and Patents Act 1988.

ISBN 978 0702 33367 5

A CIP catalogue record for this book is available from the British Library.

Printed in China
Paper made from wood grown in sustainable forests and other controlled sources.

3 5 7 9 10 8 6 4 2

www.scholastic.co.uk